Wampanoag Traveler

Being, in Letters, the Life
and Times of Loranzo Newcomb,
American and Natural Historian

A Poem by Brendan Galvin

LOUISIANA STATE UNIVERSITY PRESS
Baton Rouge and London   1989

Copyright © 1986, 1987, 1988, 1989 by Brendan Galvin
All rights reserved
Manufactured in the United States of America
First printing
98 97 96 95 94 93 92 91 90 89   5 4 3 2 1

Designer: Sylvia Malik Loftin
Typeface: Trump Mediaeval
Typesetter: G & S Typesetters, Inc.
Printer: Thomson-Shore, Inc.
Binder: John H. Dekker & Sons, Inc.

Library of Congress Cataloging-in-Publication Data

Galvin, Brendan.
    Wampanoag traveler : being, in letters, the life and times of
Loranzo Newcomb, American and natural historian : a poem / by
Brendan Galvin.
    p.   cm.
    ISBN 0-8071-1541-X (alk. paper).—ISBN 0-8071-1542-8 (pbk. : alk. paper)
    I. Title.
PS3557.A44W36   1989
811'.54—dc19
                                                            88-31447
                                                                 CIP

Thanks are due the editors of the following periodicals, in which sections of this poem originally appeared in slightly different versions: *Ascent, Chelsea, Georgia Review, Northeast Magazine, Pacific Review, Pomona, Prairie Schooner, Texas Review,* and *Tri-Quarterly.* Part I, under the title "An American Naturalist Writes to a Londoner, 1758," originally appeared in *The New Yorker.*

Thanks to the National Endowment for the Arts for a Creative Writing Fellowship and to Central Connecticut State University for a sabbatical semester, both of which helped make this poem possible.

The paper in this book meets the guidelines for permanence and durability of the Committee on Production Guidelines for Book Longevity of the Council on Library Resources. ∞

For Peter and Eleanor Donovan

Wampanoag Traveler is based on some of the surviving correspondence of the eighteenth-century American natural historian Loranzo Newcomb, a self-taught "pilgrim forager," as he styled himself, who gathered seeds, botanical specimens, and fauna for the gardens and collections of patrons in England. Although virtually nothing is known of his personal life beyond what is conveyed in his letters, he appears to have been active during the first quarter of the 1700s and to have traveled through both the northern and southern colonies while based in an area of New England inhabited by the Wampanoag tribes. I have tried to remain true to the spirit and flavor of his life, which proceeded in a time very different from ours and in the light of a world view we can but slightly understand, in which science and superstition were interlocked and the America beyond the Atlantic coast was truly a dark continent.

B.G.

Wampanoag Traveler

I

Now I will tell you our manner
of gardening here, which progresses
not by calendar, but by natural signals.
On a clear March night, I sight down
the Dipper's bowl for a backwards
question mark, tail of the rising Lion,
and then may be found slapping mud
from the plot into balls, squeezing
to test for water content, this before
even a single mallard clacks from
the creek, and last year's pumpkins
seem the wreckage of its quarter moons.
Then the whole plot is already staked
in my head, minus slugs, borers,
hornworms, loopers, beetles and all
that plague I forget each year
until they descend like a host of
savages to be bought off
only by a feast of this or that leaf,
and dug out of vines and stems
where they poke without welcome.
Asparagus I intercrop with parsley,
since I have discovered they agree
with one another. The latter germinates
long, and is said to go to the Devil
and back nine times ere it breaks
the soil, but I have found it mild
and without evil influence. Beans
I keep far from onions they can't
abide, and basil, which breeds

a merry heart, I grow along borders
with umbelliferous dill, whose leaves
are agreeable with fish, though of
a strength not to everyone's taste.
These strong-scented herbs, with chives
and mint, may keep a barrier against
insects, though my studies here
need more attention. Native squashes
and gourds are set when the dogwood
flowers, and tomatoes during
the mayfly hatch. This conveys somewhat
our manner of gardening. I would
continue but that in the mere telling
I grow fatigued, and must ask myself why,
yearly, I engage in it with such ardor
since I am without family. For the surety
of plenty, or the images such growth
alone provides, or because I do better
with vegetable kind than human,
no easy admission, and have come to
myself more than once knocking upon
and addressing a blue squash
of five-stone weight and pebbled like
the back of an alligator? By the time
of the Perseids, when my turnips go in
for autumn, I am as weary as some
old king fighting his battle with
the sea, down on hands and knees in that
riptide of beans and cabbage splashes,
a spume of chickweed flying over
my shoulders, wishing I had never listened
for spring peepers chiming their long,
ghostly sleighrides through the dark.

II

Six foot of mingled orange, tawny,
and black, its underside leaden,
a rattlesnake I kept for study
in an empty rum keg, thinking the vapors
would befuddle him, one morning
lay in wait under that cover when I came
with a snared chipmunk, and struck
my hand, pumping green poison in.

I knew I had only minutes, so cornered
a chicken in the yard, breaking her neck
with a quick upward jerk, and with
the selfsame knife as I had hacked
my murderer to portions, which yet rolled
and snapped along the floor as though
each worked to produce its own head,
I split the hen's belly and plunged
the insulted hand into her still-working
jellies and hot lights, whereon I swear
the thing's feathers wilted and began
dropping away.

           That serpent I kicked
piece by piece to the hearthfire, and soon
began a splutter and popping of fats,
a whooshing of steam among the flames,
while on my hand the fowl, now black
as though itself roasted there,
stunk in a way the Devil was in the room.
It too I added to the fire, its vile smoke

offered heavenward, then wrapped the hand
with a plaster.

                    Along their routes
veins stood and flared to the elbow,
though I plunged the arm in a bucket of
vinegar and waited upon Fate. A tree
tingled and grew from the tips of my
fingers, swelling itself up my forearm
until with a razor I opened my palm
and let my own blood flow.

I rolled and steeped some days upon my bed,
waking at times to discover the arm itself
a mottled snake, its arrowhead buried
and drinking at the chambers of my heart.
In dreams and awake I was rolled in lowly places,
sumps of the deepest hollows, among the pulp
and lichens of tumbled, ancient deadfall,
cobwebbed, prickled with my own drenched bedding.

At times I even seemed to myself a tree,
toes feeling downward toward groundwater,
at my extremities these woody prongs,
scaled, soft-pithed, where juices
wended toward the terminal buds,
which were lapped over and sometimes
in my fevers flowered, blue-lipped,
orange at heart, or rosy and black-veined,
and again like gold-wormed feather dusters.

I was possessed at times with fears and watchings.
Then vermin drew near, their faces large
as my own, lights malefic in their ebony eyes,

each sentient hair distinct, their mouth parts working,
warning against ambulations into their kingdoms.

Some evenings I was settled with cooler moments,
and at dusk, from the swamp and beyond,
a surf of sound arose as from another village
in there. I could pick out some drunkard or
madwoman's denials, but not attach them
to the screech owl, and sounds like someone
hacking brush, and breaths blown across
the mouths of flasks.

                     I reflected how these
mortal troubles began when I listened almost
from the cradle while the yellow rail sounded,
and a flycatcher whistled, desultory. Later
I stood hours on the threshold of that
bush world, thinking the pygmy owl's bark
a pup crying somewhere, boxing the air
at the end of its tether, and one day
entered a few feet in.

                     Now at times it seemed
I wandered unattended in landscapes where maroon
leaves of the oak formed metallic masks,
and was observed from thickets by eyes cognizant
of my passage there, and heard such chuckles,
small laughter and rattling, I imagined the mice
dicing, hands pressed on their mouths.

In the few hours of clarity vouchsafed me,
I was capable of depicting the seed vessel of
a lotus, with threatening holes
where the pips were cast, and land snails

nearby, and a rubythroat in arrested flight,
grasping a serpentine branch above
a hollowed log whose sockets menaced me.

That bird stares where a green lizard
emerges from a cover of pickerelweed,
engorging a bullfrog by the head, the frog's
feet clawing air. A green miasma ran in me yet.

III
[APPRENTICED TO THE BIRD MASTER]

Trout for his fish hawk's clamp,
torn ducks, shrews, what a congeries
of the bloated and debrained
I gathered. Two autumns
I scaled trees Old Longabelly
couldn't negotiate, bringing
empty nests to earth, and more than once
a papery hornet's globe.

I was his retriever as well as cook
and pack beast, and drubbed enough
for all three when he was sliding in
his boozing can. Had you crossed us
on some trace, you'd have had to peel
your best eye to discover me

under skins and dangling corpses,
strapped about with sacks, hung with
the jug he replenished at every
settled turn in the road. Thus piled,
you might take me for a wandering
apothecary whilst he trotted ahead,
wheezing under his flintlock,
a clay pipe stuck in the bore.

Grog blossoms throve across his face
and he slowed day by day,
drawing more and more to parlors,
cozening benefactors with his
beaded moccasins and a wolf's tooth
at one ear, playing senex to young ladies,

betwixt times working from models
too long stale. Therefore
his later plates are without innocence
or belief: creation's exuberance
isn't in them, though hearsay
and foozling are, as where his blue
grosbeak graces a meadowlark's nest.

Hours in the dark he stared
whispering to his cup and to the fire.
Perhaps there he saw "the underground
castle of the swallows" he portrayed
in number 129. And though he led me
to riverbanks and trained my eye

for the cleanest streaks of ochre
and red earths, and forever wandered
off trail for a scrape of black lead
or pine-green clay he seemed
to know was there—which I'd crush
in the mortar cup and bind as demanded

with beeswax or walnut oil
when we had them, or with milk
bought on the way, or flour
and water, or yolks from any nest
I could climb to and rifle—,
though he schooled me in toning
and subtilizing and blending,

and in which roots, shredded
and boiled together, yielded
dark yellows, reds, and blacks—
one morning, aged fourteen, I woke
near Charles Town believing

I could endure my hard paymaster
no longer, without arriving
at fiddlestick's end.

For he wanted my background
oakwoods vague as clouds, my rocks
mere pedestals for his birds,
nothing to draw the eye from his
foreground glories. Unlicked cub
that I was, I could not hold back:

when mud to support his avocet
was called for, I did him an ooze
of modulated umbers and greens
he'd feel between his toes,
payment for all the sloughs I walked
to retrieve whatever life
his aim knocked from the air.

The shadows of my pebbles
lean away from the sun, and every bead's
there in my pod of wild Spanish coffee,
but those plates, inscribed to his patrons,
want the name of the boy
who waded cottonmouth waters
for the swamp snowball
that overwhelms Longabelly's greenlet.

IV

[FIDDLER CRAB LETTER TO MISTRESS MARY COLBY]

They look but partly hatched
and at a loss about
completing the job, unable
as some men to say if life
goes better outside the egg
or in, and thus, like the half-made
thoughts we live by,
they remain only half-born.
This is one such thought, and I know
if I come to this mud plain
when the creek has taken
itself off, and observe
their clicking and dodging
(and think this thought), I have been
too long about town,
and need a sanative among
the trees. Once in my life
Venus struck me, looked back
across the pubescent
scut of a doe and pointed the mocking
cornu of her ears at me
before graying deeper
into falling snow. She was
a paradigm of you, Mary Colby,
and I followed
the long way home just to see
her footprints untying
and complicating themselves where
water wrinkled around

under ice. Passing the places
where rabbits, mute
until the final moment, struck
exclamations of their emotive lives
on snow, where a squirrel
beat out its terror of being
red on white: Not this! Not me!
in all its skips and evasions,
my great feet effaced everything
but those intimations of her.
When I rowed you
down this water a May evening,
and summoned
a marsh owl for your pleasure,
answering hoot for hoot
as we drifted, the bird
sailing moth-light above the boat,
I knew by your look, beloved
Mary, that you would not have me,
but live as a nun of the frost
or cleave to some thickening cooper
or barrel-counting merchant,
though you had bespelled my spirit
as surely as the blacksnake draws
its quarry from the tree to its
unlatched jaw. Therefore this mud
is hell's floor, that Babel where
the Self lives in its armor,
trotting about, putting itself
in the way, hindering others
with its cutlass-claw. For these crabs
work no more in concert
than feathers in a breeze,

but pluck, pluck, eight-legged
lower natures, mud-colored,
loving the mud, heaping up
middens by their burrows,
scuttering in and out
and sideways like crimps
and flashmen at Horn Fair.
On some that claw attains
size and weight greater than
the body's, as might
the outward sign of some inner
warpage in a man. With this
factotum one gestures
as if offering to extricate a tune
at the drop of a coin. Another
entices a female with it
as it were the season's fashion,
buying and selling, coercing
her down the hole, whilst others
by it are tossed out of burrows
as by crab publicans. They are fierce
to the flesh of drowned
mariners, but when nothing more
than the shadow of a living hand
passes across them, will take in
their eyestalks like spyglasses.
Only here and there on the mudflat
one pauses and seems to meditate,
fumbling as if it may sense
some folly, but discards the thought
and rushes into carnival again.

V

There is one in this country
whom an army cannot make
step to roadside
or increase his pace, which is
commonly no more than
a hand-gallop. For he goes
head-down and teetering,
mincing along like a tall-heeled
trull in his cloud of
rough hair, which can be black
or brown, but is always
whitewashed along the backbone
until the tailtip. He seems of
your polecat species, though
colored more variously,
and of the size of a domestic
cat, but as wide as
he is long. His head is sharp
and snouted like a fop's,
his ears prick up and, belying
his nature, he has eyes
blue-black and childlike, and
is known to promenade
with his family, marching
sire foremost, dame behind,
and kits two and two betwixt,
as in military file.
The Abnakis call him "skunk"
and make large claims
concerning the flavor of

his meat. To stop his forward motion
you merely stamp your foot, but
should he then stamp his own
and begin a backwards shuffle
with tail erect and flirting,
shoot and strike your mark,
lest he spout a liquor on you
yellow as the yolk of an egg,
which can blind for a long hour,
and whose stink, though you wring
yourself hard and sweat
many times to the purpose,
will not disperse.
It is best then to have
business outside the villages,
since you will not sweeten for
a fortnight or more, and must travel
within an effluence
stronger than the halitus
of ten foxes. Nor need you fear
trouble from farmyard dogs or wild beasts,
who will know of your approach
hours before you arrive.
Horses so bespattered run over fences,
rocks, and steeps to roll
in water for hours altogether;
cows in such condition
stand afield unmilked and crying
for the butcher, who will not
come nigh. These skunks
snout around for grubs, beetles,
ant hills and all eggs,
so the ground is funneled

as if a drove of swine has passed,
and by night have been known
to enter houses and with ready teeth
to gnaw through powdering tubs
after the meat, whereat the inhabitants
must look without protest
lest they be spewed on.
The engine of this trouble is
a cistus or bladder holding near
half a pint, and which can be emptied
in a single squirt. I am told
that this organ, when thrown into a fire,
cracks like a musket shot but doesn't
stink. It can be obtained when
the skunk drowns in a muskrat trap,
and thus I have despatched
an agreeable Indian to provide one,
which once in hand I will ship
across the water for you.
For even in the fallen skunk
has the Creator provided
the means for his raising up.
This poisonous stuff, which is
capable of rendering a man
eight hours senseless, will later
revive the heart and work
excellent feats in cheering
the spirit, and being a powerful
ophthalmic, so enriches the eyes
when they're anointed,
that without spectacles the smallest
print may be read.
Taken inwardly or sniffed outwardly,

it cures fits, and disperses megrims
and vertigoes. When you
smell this ordure many days together,
and do not come at the reason
in discovering your corn and
hay crops ruined,
then look to the trees,
where for certain will roost
a horned owl stymied as to night or day
when he stooped
upon this delicate fellow.

VI
[A NEW SECT]

These Passionaries, as you may know,
like to lie about in their finery
and lament their condition. It is nothing
to pass a harmless bush in the country
and have it begin shaking as if
it would burst afire. Formerly you
thought some beast was making its way
through, but now more likely it's
a wretch uttering truisms ready-made
for the tablets. The air fills, all
exclamations and lamentatious vowels,
all ohs! and ahs! mingled,
a catalogue of the believer's crimes
and the most unseemly parts of
his biography. A sort of high holy day
falls sometime in the mud season,
when the March air's pine-chilled,
suffused with water, and the whole cult
leaps from hummock to hummock of snow
in their best livery, wading streams
that flee the hills from a confluence
of snowmelt dropping off a ledge.
Not one of those watery bell pulls,
either, but such a curtain
as would shrink you back to your
proper significance. They enter
that roar through damp ferns and
smoking snow and take a furious dousing.
Wings of it burst up on their shoulders
and the whites of their skulls show

where it beats down their hair.
Then begins a general confession of
failure and shortcomings, as from
a collection of drowned gargoyles.
Shaky songs splatter out of them,
and glossal nonsense, while columns
rush out their sleeves, and shoes
overflow. It beats the stockings
to their very ankles, which, by the time
they are rescued, have turned quite
blue. As for me, I find a quiet walk
across a field in seed salubrious for
shaking off encumbrances
men load upon themselves. It is useful
to stir up a flight of thin, light
membranes, which climb to the air
and are carried to other regions,
there to colonize themselves anew,
or to kick up a dust and arrive
at the far side with pollinated ankles,
gold rings which are not manacles.

VII

If shipboard rats
haven't worried this little beauty
out of condition entirely,
and it has escaped those meddlesome
sorts of sailors who jimmy shipments
with a nose for liquors preserving
specimens, you will see here
a thing which in your old world
has no counterpart. These sleep
all winter, though none among
the Wampanoags can tell me where.
In summer, when I myself so love
to nap in the influence of flowers,
I have been roused by a sudden
buzzy agitation in the bell of
a trumpetvine. At first nothing
is there, then one of these
flower birds, or bird flowers—
they are so ornamented—will fly
backwards out, as quick in
reverse motion as forward,
for they go up, down, sideways
and continuous, and can stand
upon air with only a minor arousal
of it, then brief and direct as
a shooting star proceed to
a grass-pink or trillium to siphon
fragrance through their tubular beaks,
thence perhaps to the lips
of the red turtlehead blossom.

I conclude that they live solely
upon these aromas, favoring
oranges and reds because their vapors
produce the most energy. You will
not be surprised to discover that
I have tried this airy diet myself,
and for days have gone about
without other sustenance, intruding
my nose in blooms, sniffing essences,
careful not to seal the exit of a bee
or whatever else, until my rebellious
appetite drove me to clean out
the cupboard. But would I could drive
the bung home on those fellows
in your country who pronounce upon
our stingy air and unfruitful weathers—
for here's a bird that thrives
upon them! Their own sky is but
a ceiling ringed with painted nymphs,
and could I drop one of those
shrimplings overboard, just as
a great ray is passing, its breadth
that of two gentlemen's cloaks,
it wouldn't fail to elevate
the hairs along his wretched neck.
Or if I could discover the means
of sending across to you a living moose,
its rack like a tree and so plattered
a banquet could be set upon it.
A herd of your deer could cavort
beneath its legs, and posed before it
you would make no more effect than
milady's lapdog. It is true we have

no ruins, no cathedrals, but therefore
no weight of history to wrestle
as a farmer his pasture stones,
only mountains that heave like ocean,
as fit as Sinai for receipt of
prophecy, sublime for the unfolding
of immortality, and waters upon
the landscape equal to a clear eye
in an honest face, and trees which,
were they men, would be grand
originals, models for busts
and frescoes worthy of log houses.
The specious politeness of your
enervated world we are without,
and its disguises. Would we cringe
like toads, our backs mimicking
leaves spotted with decay, not to
offend or disturb? Who meets
an American meets him square-toed,
square-faced in open air, nose out,
the prow of his countenance
broached to whatever weather.
But I am straying from my path again.
The scarlet wimple on the throat
of this bird seems black
in weak light. Other times it passes
through changes that emulate
the tinctures of those flowers it
loves best. I have watched
a female collecting milkweed silk
and down of ferns, saddling them
to an underleaf branch with stolen
spider web and the strings of

caterpillars, then implanting
this device with tree moss.
Hence the nest which I enclose,
its cup formed when the industrious
bird works her body down, fitting it
to the central mass, forming the cup
preparatory for these two eggs
or twin white beans, which are merely
seeds, perhaps more secret in
their processes, but led by the same
warmth and moisture to similar
increase of life. Mantises,
dragonflies, frogs, even
the gummy spider web are this humbird's
nemeses, though one of these
flying fractions will drive after
a crow with the persistence of
a winged auger. An early frost, too,
will stun them from the air
before they can make for winter sleep,
whereby I go about among the trees
collecting them like fruit.

VIII

As to your questioning Mr. Spragg's
whereabouts, he is here, but
in such straits as I would rather
have the hoopsnake's company,
which is said to take tail in mouth
and pursue its prey like an
ungoverned wheel, or the windigo's,
whose prints the size of barrel-mouths
I may have found dripping blood
across snow once. I hazard that
my townsmen will one day
burn Mr. Spragg out, or lead him
to the gallows, for already
they mumble necromancy against him,
and surely he is a man of skill
whose art has outrun sense,
so steeped is he in the hidden
virtues of herbs, from disappearances
among the interior tribes.
He is said to crush and smoke
dried James Town weed, wild lettuce
and wicopy in a sachem's pipe. Even
were he to bring the philtre
that would draw my Mary Colby back
and bid her lay the bundling board
on my fire and undo herself,
that there be no palpable thing
between her whiteness
and my own, I would dread his daylight
approach, draped as he goes

with a string of asarum, St. Andrew's root,
and those large, white, spongy roots
he gathers in the marshes
but will not name, or reveal
the character of. More than once
he has calmed my aching teeth with
the bark of pelletory, but latterly
he has taken himself to the dunes,
his dwelling filched of sea salvage,
away from the talk of sortilege and poisons,
and perhaps from long staring at the blues
and greens in his drift fire, sees things.
Here, as close as I can construe it,
is such a tale, one of his many:
"Of an evening I felt the old beams
dislodging from my house and sliding
seaward, finding their rightful
places in keels and stems. The drowned
fleets came home from Lofoten's Sea
and Nova Zembla, and loomed in that
sober light over the Bars, forms melting
into each other and passing through
without a mast-crack. Barely a ripple,
then they all came up shaking water
off the decks, shuddering amazed at their
new swimming, and lay off there till
the deepening of the morning star."
I attribute such visions in part
to his diet, for he looks upon all the world
as fodder, and would rather assay
the brains of a partridge than her breast meat.
The panther, he assures me, broils to
a savory competing with fresh pork,

and field mice in a batter eat like ricebirds.
The red berry of creeping poxdicaria
he brews to a tea scented cherry-like,
and accounts it a great catholicon
for ridding the body of dropsies.
Nor does he hesitate to try juices of
plants, as the tulip tree, and his walls
are hung with stalks, leaves and flowers,
drying downward. Everywhere in cloth
or birchbark packets, unmarked,
are medicines. Wings of skatefish
and others the sea tosses up
supplement his foodstuffs, and once,
when I feared him frozen to his floor,
so long I hadn't spied him about town,
I went there and he drew for me
what a beach lark spoke to him
out by Peaked Hill that morning.

IX

Mohawk corn refuses no ground:
one grain's sowing in May
means three ears ripe by
October, each of thirty grains
to a row and eighteen rows to an ear,
the planter reaping, like Isaac,
a thousandfold. This lesson is lost
to Jackman, who smears his long face
with berries of mechoacan—a dye
deeper than cochineal—the more
to appear frightening.
His beard is plaited in narrow tails
reaching to his belt, which is
tucked with pistols and daggers.
Hemp cords dipped in saltpeter
he weaves into his hair, and lit
they begin to smoulder.

Jackman steps from the trees
along my path, and scatters
my sketches of broom crowberry
through the forest. He laughs
through wreaths of smoke
as if over some tiresome duty,
then upends my pack,
kicking the seeds around,
dropping sacks in the creek,
grinding the hairy-capped acorns
of red oak under his heels.
These are a mast superior for hogs.

The leaves of its tree,
broad as those of cabbages,
would be alluring to British cattle,
firming and seasoning their flesh
better than anything growing on
your commons, its timber commodious
for houses, fencing and charcoal.

Hemlock cones he crushes,
a wood hardy as brass
for wharfing, wells and keels,
and strews seeds of that iron tree
which sinks like stone
and may be the anchorwood the Chinese
moor ships with, firing my speculation
that the Western Sea makes inroads
on the farther shores of these
countries, perhaps nearer than we know
if this tree thrives there.
Axes and saws mark the iron tree
no deeper than a grassblade's width
before surrendering their edges,
but only persevere and you have material
for bowls and dishes
which will not crack or break.

Jackman has forsworn such
determinations, and enlisted himself
in that world of night
the savages inhabit. For he eats
from the kettle at their smoky fires,
and wipes fingers greased with
their bear meat, fish, and fat
on his hair and clothes or any passing dog.

His belly and nether organs
he takes for conscience, his only
husbandry the children
randomly-bred upon their girls.

What I now send you I had
stored at home, in camphor-filled jars
to deter the mice,
in snuffboxes and gourds I varnished
against spoiling airs,
and the larger nuts and acorns
dipped in wax. Much I might have conveyed
must await further shipments.
These are but a flea-nip of all to come
from this seed-gatherer's chandlery,
but you must lift your
end of our burden by procuring me friends
who'll support my narrow searches,
for I have gone shank's nag
high and low in these countries,
since many spontaneous shrubs,
growing no taller than my ankle,
I cannot meet closely
on horseback, and my feet often
cry out against me, saying a time will come
when I must refuse to open my pack
until I can sell some of its contents.

Mr. Spragg relates existence of a berry
said to cure swoonings
and melancholy, to clarify heart
and head and bring a man
to livelier conditions upon
chewing six or twelve. These

would be beneficial in my encounters
with Jackman and others.
Not a word passed, as usual,
between him and me, as though
want of usage or his new appetites
have robbed him of speech,
and I live yet because nothing
I own is worth his thieving.
Like many here, he has stumbled
in pursuit of his own lights,
but farther than some.

There's no general remorse about firing
the woods to clear for grains,
root vegetables, and potatoes,
and this completed, since there's
no king in Israel, they resort to
angling, hunting, and drinking spirits
as though bidden to it in Scripture.
Where once a vessel standing
off these shores was embalmed
by the flowering land,
smoke some days clouds the sky
so you might think God's anger is
on the country. Torpid in plenty's
face, the people let pines
bleed quite to death
rather than stanch their incisions
to preserve the matchless turpentine.
So will they flock like sharks to
flawless, dead-straight ones, which are
taken by thousands and sold to mast
the navies of France, Spain, and Portugal,

as their resins ease friction in
the grain and are supplest for dire
weathers at sea. Greater than theft
and murder is counted the crime
of loyalty here, though hemp is plentiful
and so strong that a thread
will slice a finger to the bone.
These traitors and fellows like Jackman
would be repaid by a dance
from it, without benefit of floor.

That is my wicked thought
as I pick myself up and gather
shreds of my person and property
when his appalling laughter
has faded deep enough into the leaves.
I consider I am held in
better regard by those
whose beaded and feathered ways
Jackman's adopted, along with
their risk of starvation
when the snows drive from
the northwest. For they read
in my occupations a form of wizardry,
and leave me to myself.

X

[SOME ENTERTAINMENTS SENT WITH A GIFT SNUFFBOX CARVED FROM AN ALLIGATOR'S TOOTH]

I pray this will open prime conversations
for you, and unlock certain minds
across the water. For the alligator
truly is the length of two or three men
from its head, domed like the elephant's,
to the tail, which is flattened
rudderly and as long again
as the body it depends from, and motile
four days when severed. In water
this torso appears first as clusters
of mud, as though the beast were
born of it. But on land it is
mounted on legs like the great tortoise's,
and is horse-thick yet limber and barbed
as a two-man saw. Plated from nape
to tail-tip, it appears hacked
from the stuff of infernal regions.
My first alligator I dragged out of
a fish hawk's grasp when it was
no longer than my foot,
and trained it up on crabs and herring,
until what I hesitate to call gratitude
appeared and strengthened in its nature
at last, and I could with patience
inure it to reins and a light saddle.
After many preliminaries, I galloped
my alligator about the yard
by throwing fishes before it, overlooking

those jaws as long as my arms,
which belch blood when it ramps among
its victuals, though I soon
knew that method would not carry me far.
One morning I glimpsed a better way,
and cast out a living goose tied
to a sapling. We were off down
the Jericho road. Horses dumped
their riders and plunged into brush
to avoid that hysterical fowl
fleeing my land sharkfish, which
the Woccons named Toothed-for-Woe.
Me they called *Monwittetan-Wintsohore,*
Alligator Man, for the way my dragon,
inflating itself, squalled so it leveled
a town of the frowardest savages,
pitching their dogs like bowls on a green.
Later I rode it down the Long River
to the shores of that farther ocean,
where it led me to the cask of some
sea robbers, guarded by headless crows,
and showed me the tree-walled meadow
where I heard the woolly mammoth
bellow and stamp, and witnessed its
sweep of tusk and a strangle of
loosestrife in its great trunk.
Such tales as these I might have indited
nolens volens for the greenhorns of London,
who call the beaver a woodchuck, the woodchuck
a muskrat, adventures to fatten myself
and the plagiarists with while I sat
at my fire thirty years, apiss in tea.

But why the upwelling of pity when I see
one of these slough dogs floating becalmed
or rearing its loaf of a head
and lamenting so hotly that steam issues?
Because those eye-slits and terrible
joineries evince unpurgeable sorrow—
as though it remembered its connivance
and was yet flattened beneath the foot of God?

XI

In positing my earlier theory
I may have been amiss, and therefore
approve your silence upon it,
since not from countless nights
keeping a reed's stillness
among reeds as the day's warmth
climbed visibly out of streams
and the cold slipped into
my bones, so calcifying my feet
that they could be snapped
like parsnips, can I confirm
the heron's power of making
an *ignis fatuus* of its breast-down
for enticing its prey after dark,
lit perhaps—as I earlier proposed—
by some phosphorescent
skill drawn from a diet of fish,
or else from a capacity for
storing small electrical charges
it absorbs from water. These ambitions
for discovery may well prove
fatal, as when, recently,
rousing myself from a study of those
loitering April waters
that border paths and roads,
I felt the air draw tight about me,
and what had been distant thunder
sounded nearer at hand, as though
cliffs were cracking off
and sliding from cloud down

to cloud up there. Then in rain
the air was ajump with tap roots
of lightning. Whole systems
flashed between sky and earth,
and bedrock leapt beneath my feet.
I dared not move, for as in that moment
when the bear rises among
the blueberries and attends you,
do you run or hold ground, or take
to the nearest tree? Choose
your authority, though having seen
where lightning moled beneath the earth
and dashed an oak to kindling,
I kept to the one spot, reasoning
that I would visit more points
of entry for those charges
if I rushed about. The quick,
whipping cloudburst done,
and soaked to the marrow, I looked
where sunset now spilled hues
no mortal painter could mix:
bird-yellows, tincture of
mullein-flower, still others of such
delicacy one would discover them
only on the eggs of mallard
and grass finch, perhaps
peregrine falcon and hooping swan.
But read on, Sir, forgiving my divagations
when the point in course arrives.
With the snuffing of that light
came a deep, spring-evening green,
and among titmice and blackbirds
speaking from the marshes,

one at a time petitioning sleep,
arose the needier beseechments
of male frogs. Then, without notice,
almost at each step, I was leapt against
by something, which soon I discerned
to be more frogs. Hundreds,
dropulous with eggs and heading
blindly for those waters. They were rugose
to the touch, their red eardrums
and black lateral stripes lit
by the moon. They plopped
like wet, ocellated sacs,
their ringed eyes bulging from cranial knobs,
straining as if to leap across
some gulf. Long after I gained
higher ground their ructions and snorting
continued, driven as I suppose
by that lightning's influence, which
broke them from their muddy
hibernaculum. Tell me your thoughts
upon this matter. Your interest in
things electrical I know,
and would gladly, should you sponsor it,
present my hypothesis to the Royal Society
in writing: for if that golden farina
which dusts the waters
after spring showers is truly
brimstone the thunder makes, so much
it resembles and reeks of sulphur,
is it not possible that such electric
pulses awaken the season, startle
seeds and open buds and set off
those watery copulations?

XII

I do not believe, as some here,
that the Finns of this region
make storms with their
supposed witchcraft, for they
seem a mild enough, blond people.
Weather will not be charmed,
though clearing the forests
for planting may somehow
ignite changes. Nor do I mean
to include in our ways of
prognosticating such homely
signs as the night arrival of geese
over newly-open water in
February, which yearly disturbs
an old wound under my heart,
for that is simple fact. Patches
my hound has better lore in his nose
than I in my whole frame,
for he takes the morning in,
and knows what wife is peeling
apples, and where, fields away,
the remains of a herring
breakfast may be had.
So complain my townsmen,
who drive him daily from their middens,
his path there from my door
proof enough. Perhaps he inhales,
too, news of the tide's level
at any hour, but here my
reasoning needs factual ballast.

Rain is certain when he turns
on himself more than thrice
before settling at my fire.
So too with Bramber my cat,
whom I might have called
Barometer, for the animals
feel without obstruction
what weathers will arise beyond
our scant horizons, since they
don't afflict themselves with
vanities. When she washes her face
and lies back to the fire,
next day is wet. So too
when the toad is seen at dusk,
or my chimney smoke is a column,
or spreads in this valley
without departing. My bones
do not sense rain at these times,
but I listen for crackling joints
in my chairs and table: the wisdom
pine collected from years in the air.
Each morning I consult red flowers
of the poor man's weathercock,
whose faces being open,
that day goes fair; when closed,
then otherwise. Though there be
many more, here I relate sundry
useful weather saws I have rhymed
to ease my faulty memory:

When Mistress Moon queens
in her horned crown,
the sun grins
and no rain comes down,

but when she dons
her white halo,
snow's to come,
all in a blow.

Seven stars caught in her ring
seven days the storm's a-brewing.

✼✼✼
Spider rings her net up tight,
rain by evening, rain all night.

✼✼✼
Pill-willets low above islands at dawning,
rain before dark, winds lift without warning.

✼✼✼
Six weeks before the frost will fall
the first katydid comes to call.

✼✼✼
Hornet, corn, acorn,
three things betide
hard winters. Nest
of the first
thickened, thickened
husk of the second,
prodigal crop of the last.

XIII
[A NEW-WORLD DREAM]

Nothing had ever fallen
from that sky.
Its sole angels the frigatebirds
rose outspread, feeling for lifting
motions in the air,
or anchored solitary
against the backdrop ocean clouds
which foamed and climbed
unending heights that promised everything.

Below, in a jam of masts and tackle,
men fetched the New World's
bursary aboard. As in a smashed
recessional, some dragged
the alligators, their white
dead bellies up
like those of Gin Lane tosspots.
Deer sprung from life were draped
about shoulders, and tuft-eared
spotted cats, bewhiskered,
heartsore, were hurried leashed
up gangways, and clattering armadillos.

The opossum's young
clutched her fur in terror of red
Narragansetts and Tuskeruros
whose chains rang among
braces of waterfowl: bullnecks
and black-headed whistlers,
runners, flusterers and sea pies.

Then tuns of drumming pearmains
and leathercoat apples,
hurtberries, even king crickets and butterflies
in woven cages. The while
a botany I did not know
whispered from bales and panniers,
species the years might hand down
to me, as ladystem, marsh eelplume,
the common wingtip,
and seamary, mat oakbur,
sheep-ear and eulalia, all I might yet
uncover in my foraging,
even *Erigeron newcombia*,
which I heard on the edge of waking,
and knew I wouldn't live to see
if I kept up my pilfering
this New World for the Old.

XIV
[ENVOY]

I set out
to taste of those thousands
the peddlers gloried over,
apples they said
were strawberries to the nostrils
but sour in the eating,
or hinted of fennel,
or were best at the moment
when green
pales to yellow on the skin,
or the seeds darken,
or the natural waxes surface—
meaning October, when sun
relents and the fruit is racy,
stained with September evenings,
already rusted by fogs, or hangs
purple as ram's horn
where a seed
dropped in an ox turd
took its chances,
sprouted stubborn with thorns
in a far pasture corner, the buds
partridge-trimmed until
there shoved from a juicy
reservoir the one true scion.
I passed up new-grafted whips
for old trees fighting through
lichen and scale, —ones
the deer beat a path to

by nose alone—and ate
off the knife from fonts of earth
returning to earth, savoring
local names: the Flavin Surprise,
the Cheek-in-Bloom. You,
in your century, will have
Red Delicious, Granny Smiths,
and a few other perfections
for the eye, but mush
on the palate, cores a dog
rejects by ear for their
want of snap. They will be
fenced against wanderers
like me, and warehoused away,
gassed atrocities, waxwork
celebrities, but no Oneida
Sheepnose or Wethersfield
Beauty, no Garrett's Christmas
Revenge, nothing that has a story
with it, nothing to resurrect
papillae on the tongue
like that apple I found
in a wheelrut once, browned
by November frost,
and thawed in my pocket
and robbed of such wine
the northern lights swam in my eyes.